14550 EN 921 San ES
Deion Sanders: Star Athlete

Savage, Jeff
B.L.: 5.2   MG
Points: 2.0

14560

W9-AHF-893

ES

Deion Sanders

Additional Titles in the Sports Reports *Series*

Andre Agassi
Star Tennis Player
(0-89490-798-0)

Troy Aikman
Star Quarterback
(0-89490-927-4)

Roberto Alomar
Star Second Baseman
(0-7660-1079-1)

Charles Barkley
Star Forward
(0-89490-655-0)

Jeff Gordon
Star Race Car Driver
(0-7660-1083-X)

Wayne Gretzky
Star Center
(0-89490-930-4)

Ken Griffey, Jr.
Star Outfielder
(0-89490-802-2)

Scott Hamilton
Star Figure Skater
(0-7660-1236-0)

Anfernee Hardaway
Star Guard
(0-7660-1234-4)

Grant Hill
Star Forward
(0-7660-1078-3)

Shawn Kemp
Star Forward
(0-89490-929-0)

Mario Lemieux
Star Center
(0-89490-932-0)

Karl Malone
Star Forward
(0-89490-931-2)

Dan Marino
Star Quarterback
(0-89490-933-9)

Mark Messier
Star Center
(0-89490-801-4)

Reggie Miller
Star Guard
(0-7660-1082-1)

Chris Mullin
Star Forward
(0-89490-486-8)

Hakeem Olajuwon
Star Center
(0-89490-803-0)

Shaquille O'Neal
Star Center
(0-89490-656-9)

Scottie Pippen
Star Forward
(0-7660-1080-5)

David Robinson
Star Center
(0-89490-483-3)

Barry Sanders
Star Running Back
(0-89490-484-1)

Deion Sanders
Star Athlete
(0-89490-652-6)

Junior Seau
Star Linebacker
(0-89490-800-6)

Emmitt Smith
Star Running Back
(0-89490-653-4)

Frank Thomas
Star First Baseman
(0-89490-659-3)

Thurman Thomas
Star Running Back
(0-89490-445-0)

Chris Webber
Star Forward
(0-89490-799-9)

Tiger Woods
Star Golfer
(0-7660-1081-3)

Steve Young
Star Quarterback
(0-89490-654-2)

Michael Jordan
Star Guard
(0-89490-482-5)

Jim Kelly
Star Quarterback
(0-89490-446-9)

Jerry Rice
Star Wide Receiver
(0-89490-928-2)

Cal Ripken, Jr.
Star Shortstop
(0-89490-485-X)

SPORTS REPORTS

Deion Sanders

Star Athlete

Jeff Savage

ENSLOW PUBLISHERS, INC.

44 Fadem Road   P.O. Box 38
Box 699   Aldershot
Springfield, N.J. 07081   Hants GU12 6BP
U.S.A.   U.K.

Library of Congress Cataloging-in-Publication Data

Savage, Jeff, 1961-
    Deion Sanders : star athlete / Jeff Savage
        p. cm. — (Sports reports)
    Includes bibliographical references (p.) and index.
    Summary: Provides details and statistics on the vigorous football and base-
ball careers of Deion Sanders.
    ISBN 0-89490-652-6
    1. Sanders, Deion—Juvenile literature. 2. Football players—United
States—Biography—Juvenile literature. 3. Baseball players—United States—
Biography—Juvenile literature.
[1. Sanders, Deion. 2. Baseball players. 3. Football players.
4. Afro-Americans—Biography.] I. Title. II. Series.
GV939.S186S29 1996
796.332′092—dc20
[B]   95-24332
                                                CIP
                                                AC

Printed in the United States of America

10 9 8 7 6 5 4

To Our Readers:
All Internet addresses in this book were active and appropriate when we went to
press. Any comments or suggestions can be sent by e-mail to Comments@enslow.com
or to the address on the back cover.

Illustration Credits: Connie Knight, pp. 18, 22; Rich Pecjak, pp. 8, 10, 14,
37, 41, 52, 71, 78, 81, 83, 86, 88; Greg Rust, pp. 32, 48, 76; Joe Sebo, pp. 59,
61, 64, 68; Felix Senquiz, p. 93.

Cover Photo: AP/Wide World.

Contents

1 Hard Feelings 7

2 Sports Fanatic 16

3 Two-Sport Seminole 28

4 Turning Pro 45

5 Prime Time in Atlanta 55

6 A Most Excellent Adventure . . . 63

7 Two New Starts 75

8 Superstar 89

Notes by Chapter 94

Career Statistics 99

Where to Write 100

Index 101

Chapter 1

Hard Feelings

Deion Sanders could hardly wait for the football game to start. He was wearing the red and white uniform of his new team—the San Francisco 49ers.

The 49ers were about to play the Atlanta Falcons. Deion knew all about the Falcons. He had played his first five years of pro football with them. Deion always thought his Falcon teammates liked him. But all week they had been making cruel comments about him.

Vinnie Clark was the first Falcon to speak out. "All the rest of us were in Deion's shadow," Vinnie told newspaper reporters a few days before the game. "It's a weight off everybody's shoulders that he's gone."

Deion was surprised at Vinnie. "This guy lives right behind me," Deion said, "right directly behind

Deion Sanders was anxious about playing his first game as a San Francisco 49er against his old team, the Atlanta Falcons.

me, in the home behind me. We were close. I could yell out my back door, and Vinnie could answer."[1]

Maybe Vinnie was angry at Deion for leaving the Falcons. Maybe that was it. Deion yearned for a chance to play in a Super Bowl. He thought the 49ers had a good chance of making it. So he signed with the 49ers for the 1994 season.

Deion was a great football player, no one doubted that. But he was best known for his strutting and celebrating after scoring a touchdown or making a big play. He was so flashy he had *two* nicknames—"Neon Deion" and "Prime Time." Maybe the Falcons were jealous.

Running back Craig "Ironhead" Heyward, who was new to the Falcons, was the next player to criticize Deion. "This is a new team," Heyward said. "We got rid of some things. It's not a one-man show anymore like it used to be, when they'd go out and do this little prime-time thing."

Deion was stunned. "That guy doesn't even know me," he said. "I don't think we even met before. This stuff is crazy, man."[2]

At least wide receiver Andre Rison wasn't saying anything bad. Deion could always count on Andre. They were best friends.

But three days before the game, Andre spoke out. "Deion going to San Francisco might be one of

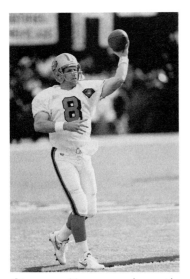

Steve Young is the quarterback of the San Francisco 49ers. After years in the shadow of Joe Montana, Young emerged as a star.

the best things ever to happen to this team," Andre told reporters. "People acted as if Deion was our savior."

Deion was terribly hurt. "I don't understand it," he admitted. "It's tough for me to handle. But I've got nothing but love for Andre and all those guys on the team."[3]

Now the game was about to begin. Deion hadn't even said hello to his ex-teammates during warm-ups. He wanted nothing to do with them. He just wanted to play football.

The 49ers got the ball first and drove smartly down the field for a touchdown. Steve Young completed every pass he threw, including a 17-yarder to John Taylor, a 16-yarder to Jerry Rice, and a 10-yarder to Ricky Watters for the score.

Now it was Atlanta's turn. Deion trotted onto the field with his new 49er teammates. His job on defense each week is to guard the opposing team's best wide receiver. For the Falcons, it would be Andre Rison.

Deion kept thinking about Andre's comments. He felt betrayed. And he was mad. He even told a reporter before the game, "I would love for everyone else to get off the field so Andre and I could just go at it one-on-one."[4]

The Falcons ran two plays for 9 yards. It was

third-and-one. Ironhead Heyward took a handoff and was hit hard by defensive tackle Bryant Young and linebacker Todd Kelly. The blow caused a fumble. Safety Tim McDonald scooped up the ball and raced 49 yards for a touchdown. Doug Brien kicked the extra point to give San Francisco a 14–0 lead.

The Falcons fared better on their next possession. They moved across midfield and into 49er territory. But Andre Rison was no help. He couldn't shake free of Deion's tight coverage. Quarterback Jeff George looked several times in Andre's direction, but didn't dare throw a pass his way. Without Andre, the Falcons eventually were stopped again. They had to punt the ball.

The 49ers rolled down the field again as Young riddled the Atlanta defense with passes. He completed one to tight end Brent Jones, another to Watters, and then connected with Rice on a 32-yarder. Finally, he threw a bullet to Rice at the sideline for another touchdown. The extra point made it 21–0.

The fourth-largest crowd in Georgia Dome history booed loudly. This was an important game—for first place in the NFC West. The Falcons had been to the playoffs just once in twelve years. The 49ers had won four Super Bowls during that stretch. The Atlanta fans were tired of watching the

49ers win every year. It was especially aggravating now that Deion Sanders, the most popular player in Falcons' history according to a survey, was helping beat them.[5]

The Falcons finally moved into position for a score. At last, Andre caught his first pass. It was a dinky 3-yarder. On the next play, Andre burst off the line, and Deion accidentally poked him in the eye. Andre was angry and frustrated.

Andre charged forward on the next play and slammed his forearm into Deion's neck. Without thinking, Deion grabbed Andre's jersey and punched him in the helmet with his left hand one, two, three, four, five times. Andre slammed his fist into Deion's helmet several times. They stood there, two close friends, fighting like young children. Officials rushed in to break it up. "C'mon!" 49ers cornerback Eric Davis yelled at Deion, "Keep your head. Keep your head!"[6]

"They should be thrown out of the game, both of them," television announcer Matt Millen said.[7] But both players were allowed to remain in the game.

The Falcons kicked a field goal to make the score 21–3.

Atlanta moved the ball downfield again on its next possession and reached the San Francisco 9-yard line. Maybe it would be a close game, after all.

Deion was upset about fighting with Andre. Now he was upset that the Falcons were coming back. It was time for him to do something about it.

Andre broke toward the middle of the field at the snap of the ball. Deion drifted with him. Ricky Sanders, another Falcons receiver, ran a short pattern to the sideline. Deion watched quarterback Jeff George's eyes. He saw the quarterback look toward Ricky Sanders.

Deion shot forward just as the ball was thrown. He stepped in front of Ricky and snatched the football out of the air. Then he took off.

The 20-yard line, the 30, the 40 . . . up the Falcons' sideline Deion raced with the ball. He held it out for all the Falcons standing on the sideline to see. At midfield, he glanced back to see that no one could catch him.

The 40, the 30 . . . down the sideline Deion went, looking over his right shoulder at his former teammates. He began high-stepping at the 20. Then he put his hand behind his helmet in his familiar celebration pose. Then he crossed the goal line for the touchdown.

In the end zone, Deion danced and gyrated. The Falcons were frozen on the field. The crowd was stunned. The 49ers mobbed Deion at the goal line. Linebacker Todd Kelly was the first to reach him.

Deion goes up for an interception.

"That's what we need baby!" Kelly screamed. "You the man!"[8]

The Falcons were devastated. They never scored again. The 49ers won in a rout, 42–3. Deion had accomplished what he had hoped to. He had returned to the Georgia Dome and embarrassed his former teammates.

"This is my house!" Deion announced after the game. "I built it, and this will always be my house!"[9]

As Deion walked off the field, he approached Andre Rison. He put his arms around his friend and hugged him.

Deion apologized for fighting at the post-game press conference. "We shouldn't let ignorant things interfere with our relationship," he said. "We'll be done with this sport in a few years, but we'll have relationships and friendships forever. You don't want to ruin them over a game."[10]

Chapter 2

Sports Fanatic

Game time was drawing nearer and nearer. The sun was out and the air was dry. It was a perfect day for baseball. Deion was so excited, he could hardly lie still on the couch.

Deion had been bugging his mother, Connie, for months to play T-ball. "Am I old enough yet to play baseball, Mama?" Deion would ask. "Am I old enough yet?"

"No, Deion," his mother would answer. "Not yet."

Finally, one day, Deion heard the words he had hoped for. "You're five years old now, Deion," his mother told him. "That means you're old enough to play T-ball."[1]

So Deion played T-ball every week. In four short weeks, he had learned plenty of the rules. He thought about them again as he lay on the couch, waiting for his mother to drive him to the baseball field.

He remembered the first time he had hit the ball off the tee. Everyone yelled "Go, Deion! Run!" and he did just as they said. He ran down the line, reached first base, and kept right on running down the right-field line. Everyone roared with laughter.

As soon as Deion learned to run the bases, he became one of the best players on coach Ted Fererra's team. His best talent was his speed. On ordinary hits, good for a single for most players, Deion would reach *second* base. And if he clobbered the ball, Deion could make it to third, and sometimes clear to home plate.

"Okay, Deion," his mother said as she entered the front room, "It's time to go to the field."

Deion popped up with a big smile. His baseball mitt was on his right hand. Deion is a lefty.

"Deion was a sports freak," his mother says now. "He just had to be playing sports. He didn't care what sport it was. Just so long as he had a ball in his hands."[2]

Deion was born in Fort Myers, Florida, on August 9, 1967. He lived alone with his mother until he was seven years old. His parents divorced when he was two, but he still spent plenty of time with his father, Mims Sanders.

Young Deion Sanders played baseball in a cemetery across the street from his parents' house.

Deion and his mother lived on the second floor of a housing project in Fort Myers, Florida. Deion's grandmother, Hattie Mims, helped care for Deion while his mother worked two jobs.

When Deion was seven, his mother married a man named Willie Knight. Deion moved with them into a blue and white house on Henderson Street near the project.

Deion played basketball at the Boys Club on Blount Street. He played football with his childhood pal, John Cummings, on the cement in front of the project. And he played baseball across the street in the cemetery. Deion usually played pitcher.

One afternoon in the cemetery, Deion and his friends got bored pitching the baseball and decided to pitch bricks. An old, vacant house stood in a rundown lot next to the cemetery. The boys hurled bricks at the old house. They broke all the windows. Then the police arrived.

Deion's mother was sitting on her front porch across the street. She had heard the windows breaking. She watched as the policemen loaded the boys in the squad car and drove off. She couldn't see that Deion was among the group.

A short time later the telephone rang. It was Deion. "Mom!" he screamed. "I'm at the police station! Come and get me!"

"Oh, you are, eh Deion?" his mother answered. "Well, let me speak to the officer.

"Hello, officer? Do you have a jail cell down there? You do? Good. Put Deion in it. I'm going to be a little late coming."

One by one, the other boys were picked up by their parents. Soon Deion was the only boy left. He sat in the cell and waited. And waited. And began to cry.

Finally, several hours later, his mother showed up. "Mama," Deion blurted between sobs, "I thought y'all forgot me."[3]

That lesson helped teach Deion to respect the law. He grew up in an area rife with drugs and crime, but he did his best to steer clear of it. Some of Deion's friends got mixed up in drugs—but not Deion. Today he refuses even to drink alcohol. As a professional athlete, Deion recognizes the importance of taking good care of his body.

Deion learned plenty of lessons while growing up. When he was seventeen, his mother bought him a moped. One night she told him it was too late to ride it. Deion got hot-headed and announced, "I don't have to listen to you. I'm gonna move out!"

Deion grabbed some of his clothes and jumped in the family car.

"No, Deion," his mother said. "*I* bought that car. That's my car. Give me the keys."

FACT

Deion had a house built for his mother in South Fort Myers, Florida. The custom-built home has two stories, seven bedrooms, seven bathrooms, a game room, and a pool. Deion has his own room upstairs that he stays in when he visits with his mother. Etched in the door of Deion's room, in 24k gold capital letters, are the words "Prime Time."

Deion climbed out of the car and angrily handed his mother the keys. Then he hopped on his moped.

"No, Deion," his mother said. "*I* bought that moped. Give me the keys."

Deion left the house walking. He stayed at his friend Hinton Battle's house. He didn't come home for a week. Finally, his mother called police captain Morgan House. Morgan's son, David House, was Deion's baseball teammate.

Deion's mother asked Captain House to pick up Deion and drive him home, and to tell him that he would be locked in a jail cell if he didn't come home every evening by six o'clock. The plan worked. From that night on, Deion came home by six o'clock.

Sometimes Captain House would show up at the ballpark. "How are you doing, Deion?" the policeman would ask. "I'm just fine," Deion would answer. "I'm coming home every night before six o'clock. I really am."[4]

Since Deion was careful to obey the law, he had plenty of time to concentrate on sports. He played Little League baseball every spring and summer. In most games, he pitched.

The Kansas City Royals played their spring training games nearby, and Deion didn't miss a game. He would take his baseball mitt to school and plead to skip out of class early. "Miss Kegley," Deion would say to his teacher, "if you let me leave early, I'll bring you back a baseball."

Deion would stand with other kids behind the home run fence and catch batting practice homers. He would get the players to autograph the balls. Then he would sell the balls for $5 or more.

Deion's third-grade teacher, Margaret Kegley, remembers Deion being a good student. "He was always neat in his schoolwork and appearance," she says. "And, of course, Deion was a whiz on the playground."[5]

Deion was a whiz on the football field as well. He began playing Pop Warner football at the age of seven when he joined the Fort Myers Rebels. Since he was the fastest player on the team, Deion played running back, defensive back, and kick returner.

The strutting of Prime Time emerged the following year when Deion returned a punt for a touchdown. "I was so excited," Deion remembered, "that when I got to the end zone, I did some stupid little step. Everyone laughed."[6]

When Deion was ten, the Rebels played in a national championship tournament in Atlanta, Georgia. Deion's team won the title game in the Dynamite Division. Deion scored two touchdowns in the game.

Deion played football for the Fort Myers Rebels in the local Pop Warner league.

Deion enjoyed playing for the Rebels so much that instead of joining his high school team as a freshman, he continued to play Pop Warner football. He joined the North Fort Myers High football team as a sophomore. It turned out to be a mistake. Deion never got to play.

"Deion was the skinniest, shrimpiest little kid you'd ever want to see," North Fort Myers coach Wade Hummel said. "He was a good athlete with a feisty attitude, but he was just so skinny. We thought he was too small to help our varsity team."[7]

North Fort Myers didn't have a junior varsity team, so Deion had to play on the scout team. He never got to play in the Friday night games. It was devastating for him. He knew he was good. Why wouldn't the coach just let him play?

Deion displayed his athletic skills on the basketball court and the baseball diamond. He played guard on the basketball team and averaged nearly fifteen points a game as a sophomore. He played several positions in baseball, including pitcher, shortstop, and outfielder.

In a basketball tournament at St. Petersburg, Florida, Deion made a play that will always be remembered by those who saw it. The Red Knights were playing Lakewood High when a Lakewood player made a steal and began dribbling toward the basket. Deion was at midcourt when he saw what happened. He raced after the Lakewood player. As the player went up for a layup, Deion came flying through the air. The ball was more than a foot above the rim when Deion pinned it to the backboard.

Deion was still small in size as a junior. But he was so fast that Coach Hummel couldn't keep him off the football field. Deion got to play cornerback. He wore jersey number 10.

North Fort Myers lost its first four games. The following week at rival Charlotte High, they scored two early touchdowns to take a 14–0 lead. But Charlotte came back. The Red Knights' opponent was driving for a score late in the first half when Deion saved the day. He intercepted a pass at the two yard line and took off. He sprinted to the left sideline, reversed field, faked past several opponents, and raced all the way downfield for the score.

Deion's touchdown gave the Red Knights a 20–0 lead. They went on to win the game. It was the team's only victory of the year.

The following season, Coach Hummel decided to change the offense. He switched to a running scheme called the wishbone. It takes a smart, swift quarterback to direct a wishbone offense. Coach Hummel named Deion his new starting quarterback.

The offense was practicing the wishbone

offense one day before the season began when Deion got creamed by three defenders. He jumped up and yelled, "C'mon! Will you guys block once in a while!"

Coach Hummel whistled for a timeout. "Deion, come over here," the coach said. Deion hustled over.

"Listen, Deion," Coach Hummel said softly, "Never be negative to your teammates. You want them to be happy to block for you. They're on your side. You need to keep it that way."

Deion nodded in agreement. He understood. "Yes, sir," he said.[8]

Deion and the Red Knights used the wishbone to march to a winning record. Deion passed for 839 yards on the season and rushed for 499 more. He gained 133 yards on the ground in one game. He returned three interceptions for touchdowns.

Late in the season, the Red Knights were losing 14–13 late in a game against Naples High when they took possession at their own 3-yard line. Naples had been stopping the wishbone offense. Deion huddled with his teammates in the end zone, then lined up as a wide receiver. It was a surprise switch. Tony Myrick lined up at quarterback.

The Red Knights moved the ball through the air. Deion made 5 receptions on the drive. The last one was the biggest. The Red Knights reached the

Naples 32-yard line with forty seconds to go. Deion ran a post pattern. He was double-teamed. The pass sailed high toward the end zone. Deion leapt between the defenders to make a spectacular touchdown catch. North Fort Myers won the game, 19–14. The Red Knights finished their season with a 7–3 record.

Deion was just as exciting on the basketball court. He averaged 24 points per game and was named to the all-state basketball team. Deion passed well and had an accurate long-range shot, but he was best known for his electrifying dunks. During one game in which he scored 30 points, Deion was making so many dunks that his teammate, Richard Fain, began calling him "Prime Time." When the game ended, Richard announced that Deion's new nickname would be "Prime Time." Deion laughed. The nickname stuck.

As a senior in baseball, Deion had an on-base percentage higher than .400. He stole 24 bases and was named to the All-State baseball team. Deion also was drafted by the Kansas City Royals in the sixth round of the baseball draft. They offered him $75,000. He turned down the offer. "I'm worth more than that," Deion said.[9]

Deion wanted to play major league baseball. It wasn't easy turning down a big-league contract.

Especially since it was the Royals—the team Deion watched play as a young boy. Deion loved baseball. But he also wanted to continue playing football. And he wanted to continue his education, too. There was only one place where he could do all three: college.

Chapter 3

Two-Sport Seminole

Choosing a college wasn't easy for Deion. More than one hundred schools wanted him. They sent him letters and called him on the phone. Some recruiters came by the house. Others visited him at school.

Deion didn't look like your typical high school superathlete. He weighed just 140 pounds his senior year. Two things made him popular with colleges—blinding speed and fierce determination.

"Most high school athletes with talent don't work super hard in practice," Coach Hummel said. "Not Deion. He worked harder in practice than anyone. He wasn't satisfied with just being good. He wanted to be great!"[1]

Deion was determined to improve his athletic skills. One thing he didn't need to learn was speed. He already had plenty of that.

Deion was working out in the weight room with his buddies one day as the high school track team practiced outside. The North Fort Myers 440-yard relay team was ranked third in the state at the time. Deion watched as the speedy relay team worked on baton exchanges. Then Deion got an idea. He would challenge the track team to a race.

Deion and three football teammates—Richard Fain, Monte Kirkland, and Johnny Brown—raced the relay team. Deion's team used a stick for a baton. Deion ran the anchor leg. Deion's team won by more than fifty yards.

College recruiters drooled over the prospect of getting such a prized athlete. Finally, Deion narrowed his choices to four—South Carolina, Florida, Miami, and Florida State. He took recruiting trips to all four universities.

Deion's mother was not happy that South Carolina was among the choices. "Try not to go out of the state," she told her son. "It would be hard for me to get to your games."[2] Deion visited South Carolina's campus and then crossed that school off his list.

Deion took trips to the other three schools. He looked at the housing quarters, talked to the football and baseball coaches, and attended baseball games. "He sat in the dugout for one of our games,"

Florida State baseball coach Mike Martin said. "He was very quiet. He just sat back and absorbed everything."[3]

Deion returned home and made his decision. It would be Florida State.

Deion liked the dormitories at Florida State. He liked the weight room. He liked the baseball field. And he especially liked that football coach Bobby Bowden promised him he would play his freshman year. Deion did not want to be a redshirt freshman and sit out his first year.

Coach Bowden held true to his word. When Deion arrived on campus in Tallahassee in the fall of 1985, he was issued jersey number 2. Coach Bowden told Deion he would play defensive back. Deion wouldn't get to be in the starting lineup right away, but he would get plenty of playing time.

Deion made the most of his opportunity. As a cornerback in a game early in the season against Tulsa, Deion stepped in front of a receiver in the end zone to intercept a pass on the goal line. Then he took off. Deion raced past his teammates and the Tulsa opponents in a blur. Clear down the field he sprinted for a 100-yard touchdown. It was the longest touchdown in Florida State Seminoles history.

Coach Bowden admired the way Deion handled the football. So he made Deion his punt returner.

That decision paid off in a game against Florida. Deion was playing with a rubber cast on his wrist to protect an injury he suffered a few weeks earlier. The cast didn't bother him, though, as he fielded a punt at the Seminoles' 42-yard line, broke to his left, then darted across midfield and down the sideline for a score. It was the first touchdown on a punt return for Florida State in six years.

The Seminoles met the Oklahoma State Cowboys in the Gator Bowl. With a national television audience tuned in, Deion made 6 tackles, broke up a pass, and had an interception. The Seminoles beat the Cowboys, 34–23.

Deion's first college football season was a success. But his freshman year wasn't over yet. When the rest of the Florida State football team started spring drills, Deion began practicing with the school's baseball team. He wanted to be an outfielder.

Toward the end of practice the first day, the Florida State coaches wanted to test Deion's determination. Deion was sent up to the plate to face Richie Lewis, the team's hard-throwing star pitcher. Lewis now pitches for the Florida Marlins. Deion dug in, and Lewis quickly blew two strikes past him. Deion squinted at the pitcher with a look of intense concentration.

FACT

It didn't take Deion long to set a record at Florida State. Against Tulsa his freshman season, Deion intercepted a pass and returned it 100 yards for a touchdown. It was the longest TD in school history, breaking the record of 99 yards set by receiver Fred Biletnikoff in 1963.

Deion smacks a line drive.

Lewis's next pitch buzzed in high, but Deion didn't chase it. Then he fouled a pitch off; then another. The next two pitches were high for two more balls, running the count full to 3–2. Deion fouled off the next pitch; and the next; and the next. It was a real battle. Deion fouled off eleven pitches in all. Then he smacked one.

It was a line drive, a bullet, a screamer up the middle. Lewis knocked it down with his glove and pounced on it. Deion was racing up the first-base line. Lewis rifled a throw to nip Deion at first by a foot.

Deion had made an out, but showed the coaches plenty. "I knew right then that this guy was special," Coach Martin said. "Deion's skills weren't great yet, but his heart was there."[4]

Deion earned a starting job as the team's right fielder. In the first sixteen games for the Seminoles, he batted .333, knocked in 14 runs, and stole 11 bases. But then he suffered an ankle injury to end his season. He had to watch in street clothes as the Seminoles competed in the College World Series tournament and took second place. Deion loved the excitement of big games like the Gator Bowl, and he was determined to play in a College World Series, too.

Deion's football career blossomed his sophomore

year. Against North Carolina in the season's third game, he intercepted two passes to stymie the Tar Heels. North Carolina scored just 10 points all day, but so did Florida State. Seminoles kicker Derek Schmidt missed a 36-yard field goal with eleven seconds to go, and the game ended in a tie.

Deion made two more interceptions as a sophomore, even though teams stopped throwing in his direction. University of Miami quarterback Vinny Testaverde was asked when he was receiving the Heisman Trophy who he thought was the best defensive back in college football. Testaverde didn't recall the name. But he knew the player. "That No. 2 from Florida State," the quarterback said.[5]

Testaverde's top-ranked Hurricanes had rallied with 3 touchdowns to beat Florida State, 41–23, late in the season. But Deion turned in the day's most exciting play. Covering Miami's star wide receiver Michael Irvin, Deion bit on a fake "out" route. Testaverde made a pump fake as Irvin broke upfield. Deion realized what had happened and took off after Irvin as Testaverde threw deep. Deion was catching up to the speedy wide receiver as the ball descended. In a full sprint, Deion leapt in the air and above Irvin. Deion's elbows were pinned to Irvin's helmet as he went over him and intercepted.

"He looked like Willie Mays making that

over-the-shoulder catch in the 1954 World Series," Coach Bowden said about his great cornerback.[6]

Deion was named Florida State's defensive MVP at season's end, and was chosen to four All-America teams.

Baseball was next. Deion struggled at the plate. He hit just .221 his sophomore year, quite a drop from his average as a freshman. But as good athletes do, Deion contributed to a winning season in other ways. He played superb defense in the outfield. He stole 28 bases, causing fits for opposing coaches.

On a sunny afternoon at the Metro Conference baseball championships in Columbia, South Carolina, the Seminoles were scheduled to play two tournament games. If they won both games, the Seminoles would win the conference title and qualify for the College World Series.

The Florida State track team also was competing that afternoon in the conference championships. Deion volunteered to help the track team in any way he could, and track coach Dick Roberts asked him to run in the 400-meter relay. Baseball coach Martin agreed—and Deion's first two-sport day was set.

Deion played right field in the afternoon baseball game as Florida State defeated Southern Mississippi, 5–1. While the rest of the team celebrated on the field, Deion was in the dugout changing into his track outfit. He finished putting on his spikes, then jogged half a mile to the track to warm up.

Deion ran the third leg of the 4 x 100-meter relay, handed the baton to future NFL running back Sammie Smith who was running anchor, and watched as Smith crossed the finish line first to give the Seminoles the conference title.

Deion hustled back to the baseball field, promptly changed uniforms again, and played center field for the second game. He hammered a single to left to drive in 2 runs for the game-winning RBI as the Seminoles beat Cincinnati, 6–3.

At the College World Series tournament in Omaha, Nebraska, Deion showed why he would excel professionally at two sports. In the first inning of a big game against perennial power Arizona State, Deion drew a walk. The Sun Devils called for a pitchout as Deion took off for second base. It didn't matter. Deion was safe standing up. ASU coach Jim Brock just shook his head in disbelief. Deion was sacrificed to third, and he scored on a fly ball. Later in the game, Deion singled, stole second, and scored again. Chris Pollack pitched a shutout, and the Seminoles won 3–0 to eliminate Arizona State.

By now, the name "Deion Sanders" was

becoming well-known among sports fans. He was being featured in magazines. *The Sporting News* rated him the No. 1 collegiate defensive back going into the 1987 season. The Florida State media guide said Deion "could be the best athlete in the nation."[7]

Deion lived up to the billing. The Seminoles were 3–0 when they arrived at Michigan State in week four. Deion had read or been told that Spartans' star wide receiver Andre Rison called him an average defensive back. Deion accepted the challenge. He shadowed Rison and held him to one catch for 11 yards.

Deion's secondary mates held the Spartans to 4 pass completions all day as Florida State won, 31–3. Deion's 53-yard punt return in the second quarter set up a touchdown, and his interception in the fourth quarter set up another. The Spartans were good enough to win the Rose Bowl at the end of the season, but against Florida State they were humiliated.

Deion sounded off against Rison after the game. "He's just an average Big Ten receiver," Deion said. "I told him, 'I watched you on film, and I thought you were great. The film must have lied.'"

Later, Deion said, "If he hadn't said anything, I wouldn't have said anything."[8]

Florida State lost a heartbreaker the following

Deion gets set—ready to blanket his man.

week to Miami, 26–25, when a Seminoles' two-point conversion pass attempt was batted away in the dying seconds. It was the only game Florida State would lose all year. Still, Deion received plenty of attention when CBS television announcer Brent Musburger called him "the best cornerback in the country" and "as good a punt returner as I've seen."[9]

The Seminoles took out their frustrations the next two weeks by pounding Southern Mississippi, 61–10, and thumping Louisville, 32–9.

Then they met Tulane and all-time NCAA receiving leader Marc Zeno. Deion guarded Zeno and held him to 4 catches for 39 yards. Deion also intercepted a pass, and returned a punt 49 yards for a touchdown as Florida State clobbered the Green Wave, 73–14.

The Seminoles closed the season with wins over Auburn, Furman, Florida, and Nebraska. They finished ranked No. 2 in the country behind Miami.

Deion decided to skip baseball his junior year and compete in track instead. Did he have success? Of course he did. Deion won the Metro conference 100-meter and 200-meter titles, and teamed with Sammie Smith, Dexter Carter, and world-class runner Arthur Blake to win the 4 x 100-meter crown. Deion was named the conference's Most Valuable Performer.

In June, the New York Yankees came calling. They selected Deion in the thirtieth round of the baseball draft. Deion certainly would have been picked much higher, perhaps even in the first round, but baseball teams weren't sure what Deion planned to do.

The Yankees offered Deion a two-year contract for $428,000. Deion knew immediately what he planned to do—play baseball for the Yankees.

Deion never disguised his love for money. He wasn't about to now. The first purchase he made was a house for his mother. "Whatever I needed as a child, she made sure I had," Deion said. "Now I want to make sure she has whatever she needs."[10]

Deion played twenty-eight games in the Yankees' minor league organization before returning to Florida State for his senior year. In those games, he hit .284 with 14 stolen bases. He came away with a sense that he could someday make it to the big leagues.

First, though, there was football to be played. For the 1988 season, the Florida State media guide proclaimed Deion "the nation's most exciting and dangerous player."[11] It was hard for anyone to argue.

The Seminoles' hopes for a national championship were smashed opening week with a 31–0 blowout loss at Miami. Deion was embarrassed and angry. This was his senior year. He wanted it to be a winning season. So he took matters into his own hands. The Seminoles would not lose again.

Deion got the team going in week two against pass-happy Southern Mississippi. Deion intercepted Golden Eagles quarterback Brett Favre's pass on the second play of the game and dashed 39 yards to the end zone for a touchdown. Deion's play sparked a 49–13 rout.

The Clemson Tigers took a 14–7 halftime lead at Death Valley the following week. Deion would change things in a hurry. As he prepared for a punt return early in the third quarter, he looked over at the Clemson bench, pointed at the Tigers with his finger, and yelled, "This one's going back!" Deion fielded the punt on his 24-yard line and cut through the middle of the field past Clemson defenders. He hurdled the Tigers punter on his way to the end zone for a 76-yard touchdown. Then he struck a pose in the end zone and screamed, "How do you like me now?"[12] The Seminoles won on a late field goal.

Deion was smiling now. The following week against Michigan State, he smiled some more. Deion and fellow cornerback LeRoy Butler each intercepted a pass as the Florida State secondary

Sanders faces Shawn Jefferson of the San Diego Chargers on
the scrimmage line.

humiliated the Spartans. Michigan State completed just one pass the entire game. The Seminoles won, 30–7.

Florida State won its next three games by twenty, eighteen, and twenty-four points. Those margins of victory apparently were not large enough for the pollsters, who dropped the Seminoles from fourth to seventh in the weekly Associated Press poll. The Florida State players were angered. They figured they had to pour it on.

Against Louisiana Tech, Deion intercepted Bulldogs quarterback Gene Johnson's first pass of the second half, and the All-American speedster returned it 30 yards for a touchdown. Florida State won by the score of 66–3. Prime Time was flying high.

At South Carolina a week later, the Seminoles intercepted 3 passes and scored at least 2 touchdowns every quarter to win, 59–0. At halftime, with the outcome no longer in doubt, Deion walked over to the stands behind the Florida State bench and told the South Carolina fans they should ask for their money back.

Against Virginia Tech, the Seminoles scored 34 straight points to win, 41–14. Finally, against Florida to end the regular season, the Seminoles' defense held Emmitt Smith to 56 yards on 15 carries in a 52–17 romp.

Deion arrived at the Florida game in a white stretch limo. He knew his thrilling college football career was coming to an end. He wanted to go out in style, of course.

But there was still one more game to play—the Sugar Bowl against Auburn. Like the Seminoles, the Tigers had lost just once all season.

As usual, Deion found a way to shine. The Seminoles took a 13–0 lead on a 2-yard run by Dayne Williams and a pair of short field goals by Bill Mason. With four minutes to go before halftime, Auburn closed to within 13–7 on a sharp play. Tigers quarterback Reggie Slack faked a pitchout left, rolled to his right, and connected with Walter Reeves who was running free. Deion raced over to help out. He grabbed onto Reeves at the 3-yard line, but Reeves powered into the end zone, anyway.

The score was still 13–7 in the fourth quarter when Auburn took possession one last time. Three and a half minutes remained. The Tigers needed a touchdown. They began their drive from their own 4-yard line. Millions of television viewers around the country watched as Auburn moved smartly down the field. They reached the Seminoles' 22 with thirteen seconds left. Time for one more play, maybe two. Slack dropped to pass. He looked over the middle. Reeves broke free. Slack delivered the ball. Out of nowhere came Deion Sanders. Deion snatched the ball out of the air at the goal line. He held on for the interception. Florida State won the Sugar Bowl, 13–7.

Deion's college sports career was complete.

Chapter 4

Turning Pro

Deion entered the world of professional sports with flash and sparkle.

The NFL draft came first. Deion had impressed NFL scouts with his blinding speed. At one workout, he ran the 40-yard dash in 4.27 seconds. "I thought I was finished," Deion remembered, "when this one scout got real nasty, saying the only reason my time was so fast was because I ran in track shoes."[1] So Deion took off his spikes, put on his tennis shoes, and ran a *4.21*.

As expected, Deion was chosen high in the 1989 draft. The Atlanta Falcons made him the fifth overall pick. To Deion, it meant one thing: money. He arrived at the Atlanta airport that night to meet the media, wearing enough jewelry to fill a small shop. Sportswriter Mark Bradley of *The Atlanta Constitution* described what Deion wore:

Right hand: A ring that spanned three fingers . . . and carried the word Prime. Also a pinky ring.

Left hand: Matching three-finger ring with the word Time. Plus a gold pinky ring in the form of a dollar sign.

Right wrist: A chain link bracelet.

Left wrist: A Gucci watch and another bracelet.

Chest: Thumbing through the necklaces, Deion called 'em out: "dollar sign . . . Prime Time . . . dollar sign . . . Jesus on the cross . . . dollar sign . . . my number (2) . . . dollar sign."

FACT

Deion was one of the earliest cornerback draft picks ever made in the NFL draft when he was selected by the Falcons with the fifth pick in 1989. Deion might have been chosen even earlier if not for the great players available that year. Here is a list of the top five picks of 1989:

NO.	TEAM	PLAYER	POSITION	COLLEGE
1.	Dallas	Troy Aikman	Quarterback	UCLA
2.	Green Bay	Tony Mandarich	Offensive Tackle	Michigan State
3.	Detroit	Barry Sanders	Running Back	Oklahoma State
4.	Kansas City	Derrick Thomas	Linebacker	Alabama
5.	Atlanta	Deion Sanders	Cornerback	Florida State

Deion wouldn't discuss the money he would seek for his first deal with the Falcons except to say, "It's gonna be a lot of zeros in that contract. You're gonna think it's alphabet soup or something, all them zeros in there." Then he grabbed a microphone. "Hello, Atlanta," Deion said, introducing himself. "This is Deion Sanders, Prime Time. Live. It's . . ." he checked his watch ". . . five minutes to eight. And the thrill is here."[2]

Not for long. Before the night was through, Deion was on his way to Albany for minor league baseball. In the Double-A league, Deion was an instant hit. When he came to the plate at home games, the scoreboard would ask "What time is it?" and then flash "Prime Time!"

In late May, Deion got the break he was hoping for. Yankees outfielder Roberto Kelly had suffered a minor injury. The team needed a speedy replacement in center field. Deion was called up to the big club.

On May 31, 1989, Deion arrived at Yankee Stadium early. The Yankees would play the Seattle Mariners in a night game. Deion's name was penciled into the starting lineup. He would play center field and bat ninth.

Deion sat in the dugout before the game and said, "You sprinkle a crowd around me, and that's what I like. Then, you'll see what I can do."[3]

Deion bunts short. He played his first major-league baseball game as a New York Yankee on May 31, 1989.

Two hours later, he was standing in center field with 22,946 fans sprinkled around him. He was under the glare of the bright lights of New York. He was wearing the famous Yankee pinstripes. "I couldn't believe it," Deion said. "I'm thinking about Mickey Mantle, and about Babe Ruth and Lou Gehrig. I'm saying, 'I'm twenty-one years old and I'm really here.'"[4]

The crowd saw what Deion could do in the first inning. Harold Reynolds ripped the first pitch of the game to center. Deion dived but couldn't get it. Reynolds had a double. With one out, Greg Briley walked. With two outs, Ken Griffey, Jr., hammered a single to center. Deion charged the ball. Reynolds raced toward home as Briley headed for third. Deion saw that he could not throw Reynolds out at the plate. But maybe he could get Briley. He gunned a perfect throw to third. Mike Pagliarulo squeezed the throw and applied the tag on Briley: Out! The Mariners scored a run, but Deion thwarted what could have been a bigger rally.

The game moved along. The Mariners held a 2–1 lead when Deion came to the plate with one out in the fourth. Yankees catcher Don Slaught stood on third base. Manager Dallas Green called for Deion to hit the ball to the right side. Seattle pitcher Brian Holman threw a fastball, and Deion delivered. He stroked a grounder to second base, knocking in Slaught to tie the game, 2–2.

The Mariners jumped out to a 5–2 lead in the seventh when Jeffrey Leonard blasted a three-run homer over the left-field wall. Down by three runs with chances running out, Deion knew he had to do something at the plate to help his team.

He led off the seventh inning. Holman whizzed another fastball, and Deion lined it to right. Deion took off running and saw Mariners second baseman Reynolds knock it down. Reynolds scrambled to his feet and threw to first: Safe! Deion beat the throw.

Rickey Henderson lined a single to right, and Deion zipped to third. Steve Sax followed with another single to right, and Deion scored. Don Mattingly singled, Jesse Barfield walked, Mike Pagliarulo doubled, Juan Espinoza singled, and all of a sudden, the Yankees were leading, 7–5. They scored twice more in the eighth to win the game, 9–5.

Deion was swarmed by reporters afterward. "You get motivated just walking in the gate here," he told them. "I was pretty pleased with what I did."[5]

Deion was pleased with his performance again four days later. In the final game of a four-game series at Milwaukee, he batted leadoff in place of

Rickey Henderson who was given the day off. Henderson sat with Deion in the dugout and explained to the rookie the importance of feeling the bat. Then he clipped Deion's fingernails for him.

There was no score in the third inning when Deion came to the plate. The first pitch from Bryan Clutterbuck was a curveball. Deion turned on it. He blasted it high toward right field. Brewers outfielders Rob Deer and Robin Yount raced back to the warning track. They watched the ball sail over the fence for a home run.

Deion pumped his fist in the air as he rounded first base. It was his first major-league homer. He would never forget it.

The Yankees flooded the field to greet Deion at home plate. Henderson was at the front of the pack. But Deion didn't jump into the frenzy as he reached the plate. Instead, he knelt down. He had broken a shoelace rounding the bases, and he bent down to repair it. "Come on, man," Henderson said to the rookie. "We want to give you high fives."[6]

Deion popped up and was happily mobbed by his teammates. Back in the dugout, Deion and Rickey joked that the fingernail clipping must have been magic. Jesse Barfield came over. Barfield was in a terrible slump. He asked Henderson to clip his fingernails, too. Rickey did so. Barfield then hit two home runs in the game. Deion scored another run, too, and the Yankees won, 12–9.

Deion was having a lot of fun playing with the Yankees. But Roberto Kelly got healthy again and rejoined the lineup. Deion was sent back to the minors with high praise. "There's no doubt in my mind that he can be a major league star," said Yankees owner George Steinbrenner. "I've never seen a kid come in and do what he did."[7]

The day after Deion was sent down, he flew to Atlanta with his agent, Steve Zucker, to talk money with the Falcons. The pro football season would be starting in three months. Deion sat down with Falcons management. They made a contract offer of $3.5 million over five years. Deion stood up and walked out.

Deion played baseball the rest of the summer at Triple-A Columbus while his agent haggled with the Falcons over money. As the weeks passed, it looked more and more like he wouldn't get to play football. The Yankees recalled him in September, and Deion returned with a bang.

On a Tuesday night in Seattle, Deion smacked a home run and two doubles. The next night, in the middle of the game, Deion laid down his bat and was gone. His agent had worked out a deal with the Falcons. Deion was on his way to Atlanta. He signed a contract the next day—a four-year deal at $4.4 million.

He had missed the entire preseason. He didn't know the defense well enough yet to start at corner-back in the season-opener against the Rams. But he would return punts. He practiced Friday and Saturday.

Then, five minutes and thirty-one seconds into Sunday's game, he scored a touchdown. Deion Luwynn Sanders became an instant nationwide star.

In the end zone, Sanders intercepts a pass.

He was the only professional athlete ever to hit a home run and score a touchdown in the same week. What's more, he was a rookie in both sports. And this was his first professional football game ever.

The game was scoreless at Atlanta-Fulton County Stadium when the Falcons stopped the Rams at their 23-yard line. Here is how Falcons broadcaster Larry Munson described the action on WSB radio:

Rams penalized five. They're fourth and 12 on their 18.

Deion Sanders brought up his arms again. Just for a moment, not asking the crowd really to holler, but making a movement.

And (Rams punter Dale) *Hatcher kicks it a mile. I mean a mile.*

Deion drifts to the left.

Takes it on the 32.

Drops it!

Picks it up.

One man missed him.

Another man missed him.

Now he's goin' wide off to the right.

Deion to the 35.

40.

The 45.

The 50.

The 45.

The 40.

My God, Deion's gonna score!

My God. . . .[8]

Deion's end zone pose with hands outstretched appeared in a color photo on the front page of Monday's *USA Today*. By Monday night he was on ABC's "World News Tonight" and on the halftime show of Monday Night Football. *Atlanta Journal* columnist Mark Bradley wrote: "Never before in the (Falcons) franchise's history has one man and one moment given off such heat and light."[9]

Atlanta coach Marion Campbell was asked to describe Deion. "He's the real deal. I like this guy," Campbell said. "He's a good person. He handles himself well in the locker room. He's a devoted work guy. The bottom line is that he wants to win. How many people would've gotten here Thursday and gotten into it like he did? At first I told him I might let him return a punt or two Sunday, and he said, 'Coach, I want 'em all.' He's got big-time speed and so much confidence. He'll be great."[10]

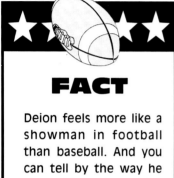

FACT

Deion feels more like a showman in football than baseball. And you can tell by the way he signs his autographs. After a baseball game, Deion will sign his full name, and make the first "S" in his last name a dollar sign. After a football game, he will simply write the words "Prime Time."

Chapter 5

Prime Time in Atlanta

Deion's world had changed. No longer did he need to seek attention. People were coming to *him* now—TV and radio shows, magazine feature stories, school appearances. Deion was becoming famous. And he had no trouble living life in the fast lane.

"Hey, all my life I be the man," he said in a cover story for *Sports Illustrated.* "I mean, I've been in the spotlight at every level. It's just a bigger spotlight. They don't pay nobody to be humble. Some people will come out to see me do well. Some people will come out to see me get run over. But love me or hate me, they're going to come out. I'm a businessman now, and the product is me. Prime Time."[1]

Still, beneath the flash and glitz, Deion was a young man viewing the world with excitement.

When former Steelers star receiver Lynn Swann

FACT

Deion isn't the first two-sport star of our era. After graduating from Auburn University, Bo Jackson played professional football and baseball. Bo played running back for the Los Angeles Raiders and outfielder for the Kansas City Royals and California Angels.

Bo became the first modern-day athlete to hit a home run and score a touchdown in the same stadium when he accomplished the feat at the Seattle Kingdome. Deion became the second athlete to do it when he homered and scored a touchdown at Atlanta-Fulton County Stadium.

visited Deion for a Monday Night Football halftime interview, Deion was in shock. "Here he was," Deion said, "right there in the same room with me."[2]

When superstar Eric Dickerson wished Deion good luck before a game against the Colts, Deion asked the great running back for an autographed picture.

Some of Deion's teammates were wary when he joined the Falcons. "Some people around here thought Deion was a loudmouth, selfish, egotistical fool," Falcons veteran cornerback Bobby Butler said. "I had to reassure them he was a good guy, just the opposite of the image."[3]

If anyone had a reason to dislike Deion, it might have been Butler. Deion took Butler's left corner-back job in week six.

Deion wasn't nervous before his first start. He knew what he could do. But did opposing teams know? The New England Patriots found out. On the second play of the game at Atlanta, Patriots receiver Cedric Jones ran a short "out" pattern in front of Deion. Quarterback Doug Flutie threw the ball. Deion batted it away. Then he put his hands on his hips and taunted the Patriots' bench.

"I was so pumped up to break up that ball," Deion said. "That's the first ball thrown at me since

I don't know when. They didn't throw at me in college. They're definitely going to throw at me at this level. I was so pumped up to see the ball coming at me."[4]

But Deion showed he wasn't perfect. In the second quarter, the Patriots had the ball deep in Falcons territory. Jones went in motion to the right. Deion followed him. Jones broke back left on a slant pattern and Deion didn't keep up. Jones caught the pass and skipped into the end zone before Deion could catch him.

It was the only touchdown New England scored. The Falcons held on to win, 16–15.

Deion graded himself afterward. "I would say a C plus," he said. "I didn't play up to the level I could play up to. But I'm learning."[5]

When the season ended, Deion took some time off to rest, and then joined the Yankees for spring training. Unfortunately, his second big-league season would be what he described as "a soap opera."[6]

Deion started the season with the Yankees, was sent down to Triple-A Columbus April 30, recalled by the Yankees May 21, sent back to Columbus June 28, and brought up a third time by the Yankees July 13. Deion left the Yankees early in September to join the Falcons, and the Yankees released him.

"Football is still No. 1 for me. It's got to be No. 1. It's making me more money," Deion said. "I'm married to football. Baseball is just my girlfriend."[7]

Deion's second year with the Falcons was just as spectacular as his first. He intercepted a pass against the Houston Oilers and returned it 82 yards for a touchdown. He returned a punt against the Cincinnati Bengals 79 yards for a score. In the last game of the season, he returned an interception 61 yards for yet another touchdown to help beat the Dallas Cowboys.

Still, the Falcons finished with a 5–11 record to miss the playoffs for the eighth straight year. Losing like this was new to Deion. But his thoughts soon turned to baseball again when the local Braves signed him to a contract for the 1991 season. It was a one-year deal for $650,000 that allowed Deion to leave the Braves halfway through the season to join the Falcons at training camp.

Maybe Deion wouldn't have to give up one sport to play the other. Maybe he could just shuttle back and forth on Interstate 85 between the Braves and Falcons practice sites. Maybe he could practice with the Falcons and play home games at Atlanta-Fulton County Stadium with the Braves. Who knows? Deion didn't. But he did know his fondness for baseball was growing.

"I see myself in the long run being a baseball player," he said. "Football will last only a few more years for me."[8]

The Braves planned to send Deion to their Triple-A club in Richmond to start the season. Deion foiled those plans. He earned a spot on the big league roster, then impressed the team with his hustle and desire. A month into the season, Deion had an on-base percentage of .333 with 4 stolen bases. "He's been as good a player as we've put out there every night," General Manager John Schuerholz said. "He's played with fire, with aggressiveness, and he's been getting on base. He worked his tail off this spring to make this team. We couldn't have asked any more of him."[9]

The hot summer rolled on. The Braves were in first place in the National League West. Falcons training camp had begun. And Deion was being fined daily for not being in camp. He had to leave the Braves.

Deion's final baseball game was at home against the Pittsburgh Pirates. Of course, Deion finished with a bang. He drilled a three-run homer to win the game, 8–6.

Two weeks later, Deion walked onto the grass at Fulton County Stadium wearing a new black Falcons jersey. And he would make news again. In a

After the Yankees released him, Sanders was concerned that he might have to give up baseball. When the Atlanta Braves signed him soon after, all his worries were over. He'd be playing for two Atlanta teams.

preseason game against the Tampa Bay Buccaneers, Deion played his usual positions of cornerback, punt returner, and kick returner. But he also joined the Red Gun offense. It was an experiment by coach Jerry Glanville. And it worked. Deion made two catches for 73 yards, including a 52-yarder in which he outjumped a defender and was tackled at the 2.

"I want to get the ball in my hands," Deion said. "I think everyone on the coaching staff knows that."[10]

The Falcons were 1–2 to open the season when things got hectic for Deion. It was late September, and the Braves were in a playoff race. The Braves called Deion and asked if he were available if they needed him. He said yes, as long as it didn't interfere with his football job.

On Sunday, he held Los Angeles Raiders wide receiver Willie Gault without a catch, sacked quarterback Jay Schroeder and forced a fumble on the play, and intercepted a pass to lead the Falcons to a 21–17 victory.

The Falcons did not practice Tuesday, so Deion joined the Braves for a game at home against the Cincinnati Reds. The game was rained out.

The next day was crazy. Deion arrived at Falcons practice at 9:00 A.M. First, he attended a special teams meeting and then a defensive meeting. At noon, he practiced fielding punts. At 1:00 P.M., the regular practice began. At 3:30 P.M., the team returned to the locker room to dress and go home—not Deion. He boarded a helicopter in the parking lot, and was flown to Fulton County Stadium for a double-header against the Reds. At 7:00 P.M., he entered the first game in the ninth inning as a pinch runner. He promptly stole second base, jumped to his feet, and pumped his fist in the air. The Atlanta crowd went berserk. They loved Deion. At 11:00 P.M., he entered the second game, again in the ninth inning as a pinch runner. This time he was forced out at second base.

Deion received a warm welcome in Atlanta. Fans loved this hard-working athlete.

Deion practiced with the Falcons the next day and joined the Braves again that night for another game against the Reds. This time, he did not get in the game. "I was hoping he'd play tonight—he's my idol," said Reds pitcher José Rijo, who shut out the Braves, 8–0. "It's not that he plays two sports, but he plays them both very well."[11]

The San Francisco 49ers saw that two weeks later in Candlestick Park when Deion returned a kickoff 100 yards to help the Falcons win, 39–34. But for Deion, that game was bittersweet. The Braves were in the playoffs, and Deion couldn't play.

Deion's commitment to football meant the Braves couldn't put him on their playoff roster.

When the Braves reached the World Series, it was especially tough for Deion. He had to watch from the standing area at Fulton County Stadium as his team played the Minnesota Twins. "Killed me," he said. "Because it was the big game. I haven't been in a big championship game since Pop Warner."[12]

Deion did get some consolation with his football team. The Falcons won six of their last eight games to reach the playoffs.

Deion was a big reason for his team's success down the stretch. He intercepted two passes to set up touchdowns against the Tampa Bay Bucs, then intercepted two more passes and returned a lateral 48 yards for a score in a win over the Seattle Seahawks.

Although the Falcons lost in the first round of the playoffs, it was another terrific year for Deion. He led the NFC with 6 interceptions. He was voted to the Pro Bowl. What he really wanted, though, was to play in a big game—either a Super Bowl or a World Series. He would get that chance.

Chapter 6

A Most Excellent Adventure

Deion was so focused on baseball that he hardly even mentioned the word *football.*

"I've accomplished my goal in that other thing," he told a reporter at the start of the 1992 baseball season. "Now it's time for me to accomplish a goal in this thing."

What is the goal?

"Success. *Enormous* success," he said. "I'm a good baseball player. But I can be a *great* baseball player. A *star* baseball player."[1]

Two weeks into the season, Deion was meeting his goal. He was batting .426, with at least one hit in each of the thirteen games the Braves had played. He led the National League in hits, extra-base hits, total bases, and triples.

"Before, he would just grab his bat and helmet and go up there and hit," Braves batting coach

Clarence Jones said. "Now he prepares himself before every game: who's pitching, what they're throwing, where they're throwing it and how they're trying to get him out. Now he's using his head along with his ability."[2]

Deion singled, doubled, and scored in Atlanta's opening day 2–0 win at the Houston Astros. A few nights later, in a big game against the San Francisco

Jeff Bagwell of the Houston Astros waits for the ball in vain, as Deion tags up.

Giants, he singled twice and scored both times in a 6–2 victory. Against the Cincinnati Reds the next night, he had 2 triples, a double, and a single in the first four-hit game of his career.

Atlanta fans loved him. In a local newspaper poll of fans, Deion was voted Georgia's best athlete, getting twice as many votes as anyone else. His teammates loved him, too. "He's incredible," pitcher Mark Grant said. "We love having him. I admit I prejudged him at the beginning. I saw him on the cover of *Sports Illustrated* and thought, 'Who is this idiot?' But you get to know him, and you realize he has a heart of gold."[3]

Steve Avery admired Deion's style of clothes so much that the Braves pitcher gave Deion $5,000 to buy him a new wardrobe. Did Deion spend all the money? "Sure. Plus another grand he owed me when I got back," Deion said. "It only took me a couple of days. I can spend money very fast, especially when it's not mine."

Avery showed up in the Braves clubhouse the next day wearing a flowery shirt and mustard-colored pants. "Now," Deion said, "he looks like a man."[4]

The season rolled along, and once again the Braves were headed for the playoffs. Football season began, and Deion proved he was ready by helping the Falcons to a 20–17 victory over the New York Jets. Then he returned a kickoff 100 yards for a touchdown the first time he touched the ball against the Washington Redskins at RFK Stadium.

But baseball was the sport on Deion's mind. The Braves were about to play the Pittsburgh Pirates in the National League Championship Series. Deion wasn't about to miss out on the playoffs again.

The Braves won the first two games, and Deion enjoyed the excitement, even though he spent most of the time on the bench. The Pirates won Game 3 on a five-hitter by Tim Wakefield.

Now Deion was worried. The Falcons had a game in two days against the high-powered Miami Dolphins. They needed Deion. The Braves were in a dogfight with the Pirates. They needed Deion.

The Falcons game was Sunday at 1:00 P.M. in Miami. The next two Braves games were Saturday and Sunday night at 8:30 P.M. in Pittsburgh. What would Deion do? What *could* he do? He couldn't play both sports, could he?

Oh, yes he could.

Eighteen minutes past midnight on Sunday at Three Rivers Stadium, Deion strode past dozens of TV camera crews and climbed into a stretch limousine. He had just played the last two innings in left field of Atlanta's 6–4 victory in Game 4.

FACT

Deion's 100-yard kickoff return for a touchdown in 1992 at RFK Stadium against the Redskins put him in the NFL record book. Deion became the first player since Hall of Famer Bobby Mitchell (1958–61) to return a punt or kick for a score in four consecutive seasons.

At 12:58 A.M., he boarded a chartered airplane at Allegheny County Airport for a two-hour, twenty-minute flight to Fort Lauderdale, Florida.

At 3:37 A.M., he rode in another stretch limo to the hotel where the Falcons were staying.

At 12:14 P.M., he emerged from the tunnel at Joe Robbie Stadium in Miami wearing his football uniform and the popular black scarf—the players call them "do-rags"—knotted over his head.

At 1:35 P.M., he was penalized on a 47-yard pass interference call on Dolphins receiver Mark Duper.

At 1:48 P.M., he lined up on offense and caught a screen pass from quarterback Chris Miller. He ran 9 yards to put the Falcons in position for a field goal that gave them a 10–7 lead.

At 4:06 P.M., he walked off the field dejectedly after Miami's 21–17 victory.

At 4:25 P.M., he received a glucose injection by the team doctor to combat dehydration caused by the ninety-degree heat in Miami.

At 4:48 P.M., he jumped into another limousine that took him to a helicopter pad.

At 4:55 P.M., he climbed into a helicopter that flew him to Opalocka Airport.

At 5:19 P.M., he boarded a private jet that took him back to Pittsburgh.

Playing two sports at once didn't give Deion much time for shut-eye. Still, he excelled in both sports.

At 7:45 P.M., he arrived at Allegheny County Airport, then boarded another helicopter.

At 8:01 P.M., the helicopter landed atop the Channel 11 building in downtown Pittsburgh. He took an elevator to the bottom, climbed in a black stretch limo, and rode to Three Rivers Stadium.

At 8:26 P.M., he arrived at the stadium where thousands of fans were lined up to see him.

At 8:43 P.M., the first pitch of Game 5 was thrown. He was in the dugout wearing his Braves uniform.

The baseball-football-baseball experience was Deion's version of a Most Excellent Adventure. The Braves lost Game 5 by a 7–1 score, thanks to Barry Bonds who singled, doubled, drove in a run, stole a base, and scored twice. But Deion's incredible two-sport odyssey was the big news of the night.

"With Deion," his agent, Eugene Parker, said, "it has to be dramatic."[5]

The Braves lost Game 6, but they won Game 7 in amazing fashion when little-known Francisco Cabrera delivered a two-run single with two outs in the bottom of the ninth inning. The Braves were going to the World Series. They would meet the American League Champion Toronto Blue Jays. The best for Deion was yet to come.

Deion only batted five times in the playoffs. He wanted more action. Manager Bobby Cox agreed.

After the Braves won the first game 3–1 on Damon Berryhill's three-run homer, Deion was inserted into the starting lineup for Game 2. It was his reward for skipping the Falcons' game that day against the 49ers.

In Game 2, Deion played left field and batted second. He drew two walks, singled, scored a run, and stole two bases. The Blue Jays rallied with two runs in the ninth to win, 5–4. But this was Deion's time to shine. This was Prime Time.

In Game 3, Deion went 3-for-4 with 2 singles and a double. And he scored a run and stole another base. But again, the Jays scored single runs in the eighth and ninth for a comeback 3–2 win.

In Game 4, Deion singled twice, drove in a run, and scored another to lead the Braves to a 7–2 triumph.

Deion was hot. He was in the spotlight—and he was delivering. For some reason, Braves manager Cox rested Deion for Game 5. It was a bad mistake. The Braves lost.

Deion was back in the lineup for Game 6. And he delivered again. He doubled, singled, scored a run, and stole 2 bases. But the Jays scored two runs in the eleventh inning to win the game, 4–3. Toronto was the baseball champion.

For the Series, Deion led all players in hitting

with a .533 average, 2 doubles, 4 runs scored, and 5 stolen bases. If the Braves had won the Series, Deion would have been the MVP.

Instead, it was back to football.

Deion was a human highlight film the rest of the 1992 football season.

He dashed 73 yards for a touchdown off two laterals at Buffalo. He knocked down 2 touchdown passes, made 6 tackles, and set a team record with 245 yards in returns at New Orleans. He intercepted 2 passes and recovered a fumble in a win over New England. And he caught his first touchdown pass on offense—a 37-yarder—at Tampa Bay.

It was Deion's performance the following season, though, that probably guaranteed him a spot in the Pro Football Hall of Fame.

Deion stayed with the Braves again through the baseball season and into the playoffs where they lost to the Philadelphia Phillies. When he joined the Falcons, they were 0–5. Their defense was allowing thirty points a game.

Deion changed matters in a hurry.

He joined the team one hour before a Thursday night game at the Georgia Dome against the Los Angeles Rams. He entered the contest with four minutes left in the first quarter as a "nickel" defender. He moved in at his familiar right

Cornerback is probably one of the least familiar positions in football. Stars like Sanders are often overlooked by the press.

FACT

Deion likes to drive into poor neighborhoods and pass out free tickets to pro football and baseball games. That's because he never got the chance to attend a game as a child.

The first regular season baseball game Deion ever saw in person was at Yankee Stadium on May 31, 1989. He played in it.

The first pro football game Deion ever saw in person was at Atlanta-Fulton County Stadium against the Rams on September 10, 1989. He played in it.

cornerback spot two minutes later. Then he batted down two passes. The Falcons won their first game, 30–24.

At New Orleans the following week, Deion intercepted Wade Wilson's pass and raced 37 yards down the left sideline before getting tackled at the 5. Two plays later, the Falcons scored the first touchdown of the game. Atlanta won, 26–15.

Five straight losses without Deion. Two straight wins with him.

"It isn't me, man," Deion said after the Saints game. "It's the guys."[6]

The Falcons disagreed. "His presence has a lot to do with it," safety Roger Harper said.[7]

"He definitely gives us a lift," defensive end Tim Green said. "He's an impact player who can turn a game around."[8]

Tampa Bay beat the Falcons, 31–24, the following week, largely because the Bucs quarterback Craig Erickson was smart. He threw 28 passes in the game. Only four were at Deion.

But Atlanta bounced back to win its next three games. First, they shut out the Rams on the road. Deion intercepted 2 passes. Then they beat the Dallas Cowboys and Cleveland Browns at home.

Against Dallas, Deion played tight coverage on

star receiver Michael Irvin and held him to one catch for 5 yards. Deion also got in the game on offense for a play. He caught a short pass in the flat from Bobby Hebert and ran through the Cowboys' defense 70 yards for a touchdown. He high-stepped down the sideline for the last thirty-five yards, the final ten with one hand behind his head.

"Hopefully you guys will write good stuff and put pressure on the people around here to let me play a little more offense," Deion told reporters afterward.[9]

Teammate Andre Rison summed it up when he said, "Deion just happens right now to be the world's finest athlete."[10]

The Falcons missed the playoffs. But they didn't give up. In an NFC West showdown with the 49ers late in the season, Deion squared off against the best receiver of all time—Jerry Rice. This would be the ultimate test. And it would also change Deion's career, although he didn't know it yet.

Deion could not completely stop Rice. The great receiver caught 6 passes for more than 100 yards, including a brilliant over-the-shoulder grab with Deion draped over him. But Deion kept Rice out of the end zone. And he intercepted 2 passes. The Falcons won, 27–24.

The 49ers were impressed with Deion—very

impressed. Rice was especially impressed. "You know what really gets me about Deion?" Rice said. "You know that strut he does when he's running for a touchdown? The one where he's holding his hand up behind his head, and lifting his legs in that goose step? Yeah, yeah, it's funny, ain't it. But did you ever notice that when he's doing that run *no one* ever catches him? Did you ever notice that Deion's *pulling away* from people?"[11]

Chapter 7

Two New Starts

Deion's life changed dramatically in 1994. He was in Atlanta when the year began—a member of the Falcons and Braves. But that didn't last for long.

First the Braves traded Deion to the Cincinnati Reds. It happened two months into the season, on May 29. It was a straight-up trade—Deion for outfielder Roberto Kelly. Ironically, when Deion first arrived in the major leagues five years earlier with the New York Yankees, it was Roberto Kelly whom he replaced in the lineup.

The Braves were 29–17 and leading their division by two and a half games when Deion was traded. When the players' strike hit two months later, they were trailing Montreal by six games.

With the Reds, Deion batted .277 in forty-six games, scored 26 runs and stole 19 bases. Then the strike hit. Then season came to a halt. There would be no World Series.

The Braves traded Deion to the Cincinnati Reds in 1994.

So Deion went shopping for a football team.

He enjoyed playing for the Falcons. But his contract was up, and he wanted to play for a championship team. He wanted to play in a Super Bowl.

The Falcons offered him $2.88 million for one year. The Miami Dolphins offered him $3 million for a year. The New Orleans Saints offered him $17 million for four years. Deion said no, no, and no.

The 49ers offered him $1.2 million for a year. He said yes.

"I'm going there to win a Super Bowl," Deion said before boarding a plane to the West Coast. "That ring is the most important thing."[1]

The 49ers had played against Deion twice each year. They saw how talented he was. The Niners had lost to the Dallas Cowboys in the previous two NFC championship games, and they were determined not to let that happen again. They knew Deion was the one player who could stop Cowboys star wideout Michael Irvin.

When Deion arrived in San Francisco, the 49ers held a press conference for him. Deion said simply, "They've won four Super Bowls. I'm here to make it five."[2]

Deion immediately went to work. In his first start of the season, against the New Orleans Saints at Candlestick Park, Deion made a huge play. With

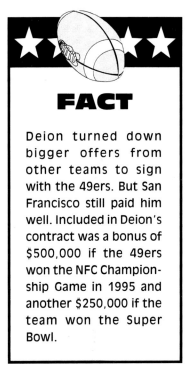

FACT

Deion turned down bigger offers from other teams to sign with the 49ers. But San Francisco still paid him well. Included in Deion's contract was a bonus of $500,000 if the 49ers won the NFC Championship Game in 1995 and another $250,000 if the team won the Super Bowl.

Deion wanted badly to win a championship. When his contract with the Falcons ended, he passed up their one-year $2.88-million contract. Instead he signed a one-year $1.2-million contract with the first-rate 49ers.

the Saints driving for the winning score, Deion intercepted Jim Everett's pass with thirty-two seconds left, and took off the other way. He ran 74 electrifying yards, high-stepping the last thirty-five of them. The crowd exploded as Deion scored. The 49ers won, 24–13.

"He may be the fastest person I have ever seen on the football field," 49ers safety Merton Hanks said. "When he made that cutback, he went from second gear to third, and he was instantly in the open. I said, 'Oh my goodness.'"[3]

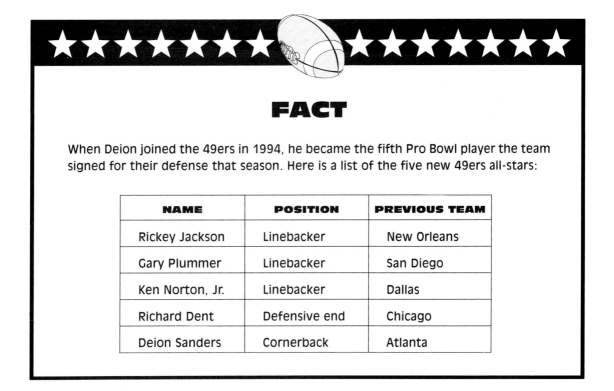

FACT

When Deion joined the 49ers in 1994, he became the fifth Pro Bowl player the team signed for their defense that season. Here is a list of the five new 49ers all-stars:

NAME	POSITION	PREVIOUS TEAM
Rickey Jackson	Linebacker	New Orleans
Gary Plummer	Linebacker	San Diego
Ken Norton, Jr.	Linebacker	Dallas
Richard Dent	Defensive end	Chicago
Deion Sanders	Cornerback	Atlanta

The 49ers lost the following week, but then they won ten straight games, including a victory over the Cowboys, to clinch homefield advantage throughout the playoffs.

Deion's presence allowed the 49ers to try new formations on defense. They didn't have to worry about his side of the field, because he would cover his receiver, and that would be that. Deion was so valuable that the 49ers didn't allow him to return punts or kickoffs, to cut down on the risk of his getting hurt. Deion didn't mind. He just wanted to play in "The Show."

What's more, Deion was having fun with his new teammates. The 49ers hammered the Falcons 44–3 in Atlanta, then clobbered them again at Candlestick Park, 50–14, late in the season. In the win at San Francisco, safety Merton Hanks made two interceptions. After one of them, he lateraled the ball to Deion who fumbled it out of bounds. Coach George Seifert hates that sort of hot-doggy trickery, and the players know it. In the locker room after the game, Coach Seifert presented Hanks with a game ball. "Here Merton," Deion called out with a grin, "lateral it to me." The players roared with laughter. Even Coach Seifert chuckled.[4]

"Everybody likes Deion. He's such a likeable guy," safety Tim McDonald said. "Everybody thought he'd be something outlandish, and everybody was so relieved that he's so down-to-earth."[5]

Deion was sky high after he was named pro football's Defensive Player of the Year. And he was even happier when the Niners trounced the Chicago Bears, 44–15, in the first round of the playoffs. Dallas would be coming to Candlestick Park the following week for the NFC title game showdown.

The 49ers knew that Sanders was an excellent cornerback, but many of the players thought he was going to be out-of-control. Instead, they found him to be a likeable guy.

"This game Sunday is the Super Bowl," Deion said. "This is why I came. This is *the* reason."[6]

The 49ers acquired Deion for this game. They had said so all season. The 49ers and Cowboys were widely considered the two superior teams in football.

The two-time Super Bowl champion Cowboys would be tough to beat. Wide receivers Michael Irvin and Alvin Harper were two of the game's best. Harper especially hurt the 49ers the previous two times at Candlestick. The speedy receiver made a 70-yard catch to set up Dallas's game-clinching touchdown in the 1993 NFC title game. When the Niners stopped the Cowboys, 21–14, earlier in the year, Harper had a 90-yard catch. He was averaging 33.4 yards a catch against San Francisco.

The 49ers coaches decided to put Deion one-on-one against Harper, and use a cornerback and safety to double-cover Irvin on the other side.

The plan worked. On Dallas's third play, just a minute into the game, quarterback Troy Aikman forced a pass toward Irvin's side of the field. Forty-niners' Eric Davis, cornerback, stepped in front to intercept the pass and returned it 44 yards for a touchdown. Just like that, the 49ers led, 7–0.

It would get worse for Dallas. On their second possession, the Cowboys turned the ball over again.

Irvin was stripped after catching a pass over the middle. The 49ers converted a 29-yard pass down the right sideline from Steve Young to running back Ricky Watters.

On the ensuing kickoff, Kevin Williams fumbled, and the 49ers recovered again. Three turnovers in five minutes. The Cowboys were shocked. The 49ers marched 35 yards in seven plays

The San Francisco 49ers are one of the most successful teams in professional football. They have won all five of their Super Bowl appearances, more than any other team.

with fullback William Floyd bursting into the end zone. Seven minutes into the game, the 49ers led, 21–0.

Deion knew it wasn't over. The Cowboys were too good. Aikman would be throwing passes the rest of the game. It would be a real challenge to hold the lead.

Dallas roared down the field to score. With Deion blanketing Harper, the Cowboys threw to Irvin. The great receiver split defenders Davis and Toi Cook to catch a 44-yard bomb in the left corner of the end zone to get Dallas back in the game. The Cowboys cut the lead to 21–7, and it was still the first quarter.

After a San Francisco field goal made it 24–7, the Cowboys scored another touchdown. Aikman completed passes to tight end Jay Novacek for 15 and 19 yards, then connected with Irvin for a 12-yard gain. Two plays later, Emmitt Smith powered 4 yards for the touchdown. The score was 24–14. The Cowboys were back in the game.

Forty-niners' wide receiver Jerry Rice responded with the biggest play of the day. With eight seconds left before halftime, Rice outran two defenders to catch a perfectly lofted pass by Young in the end zone. The 23-yard touchdown broke the backs of the Cowboys. Down 31–14 with only a half to go, they would never recover.

Emmitt Smith plowed for a one-yard touchdown early in the third quarter, but Steve Young responded with a 3-yard scoring run to increase the lead to seventeen again.

The Cowboys were frustrated. A big part of their offense was being taken away. Alvin Harper was just not getting open. Deion was guarding him too closely. On one play in the third quarter, the Cowboys desperately tried get the ball to Harper. They threw deep to him. Once again, Deion was in perfect position. He made a diving interception. The crowd roared in celebration.

Irvin caught a 10-yard touchdown pass midway through the fourth quarter, but the 49ers would not allow the Cowboys to score again. The 49ers won the game, 38–28.

Irvin would finish the game with 12 catches for 192 yards and 2 touchdowns. But Harper would catch just one pass for 14 yards. "They did a good job on Alvin," Aikman said afterward. "He's had some big games on them in the past, and they did something to stop him today."[7]

That *something* was Deion Sanders. Now Deion would get his wish—to play in a Super Bowl.

The 49ers met the surprising San Diego Chargers in Super Bowl XXIX. More than 130 million people across the country, and millions more around the

Fullback William Floyd charges downfield. Floyd captured a 5-yard pass for a touchdown in the first half of Super Bowl XXIX.

world, tuned in to the game at Miami's Joe Robbie Stadium. And from the start, there was never a doubt about who would win.

The 49ers scored on their third play from scrimmage when quarterback Steve Young threw 44 yards to wide receiver Jerry Rice who broke free over the middle. They scored again on the fourth play of their next possession as Young connected with running back Ricky Watters on a crossing pattern, and Watters broke two tackles to dash 51 yards for the score. Just like that, four minutes into the game, the Niners led, 14–0.

The Chargers answered with a score as Natrone Means busted over from one yard out. But the 49ers reached the end zone twice more before halftime as Young threw a 5-yard touchdown pass to fullback William Floyd and an 8-yard scoring pass to Watters in the left flat.

Deion had an easy first half as the 49ers' linemen put pressure on San Diego quarterback Stan Humphries and forced him to throw wildly. Deion figured he would be tested in the second half. He wasn't. San Francisco dominated the rest of the way as Young finished with 6 touchdown passes—a Super Bowl record. Rice and Watters each scored three times, tying another record.

Deion got into the action on defense when he

After the 49er victory over the Chargers in Super Bowl XXIV, Sanders shows himself to be a "good winner."

made an interception in the end zone in the fourth quarter. He even got to play on offense for one play—something that coach George Siefert *never* would have done unless he really liked Deion. The play was designed for Deion, too. Deion lined up on the right side as a receiver and ran a fly pattern. He was open 30 yards downfield, but Young's pass hung in the air a split second too long and Chargers safety Stanley Richard tipped it away.

The 49ers won the game in a rout, 49–26.

"We just beat the heck out of them," Deion said to a crowd of several hundred reporters at the post-game press conference. "They didn't have a chance. We gave 'em respect, but we knew we were going to beat them."[8]

Deion finally got his wish—a Super Bowl ring. And he accomplished one more thing along the way. He became the first athlete in the history of sports to play in both a Super Bowl and a World Series.

Chapter 8

Superstar

In 1995, Deion changed teams again. In late July, he was traded to the San Francisco Giants where he immediately became the team's leadoff hitter and center fielder. It seemed certain now that Deion would be a two-sport star in San Francisco, playing football for the 49ers and baseball for the Giants.

But Dallas Cowboys owner Jerry Jones shocked the football world when he offered Deion an incredible $35-million contract to join the Cowboys. No defensive player had ever been offered so much money. The contract was for seven years, and Deion would be paid $13 million as a bonus, just for signing his name. Deion loved playing for the Super Bowl champion 49ers, but how could he refuse so much money? He couldn't.

Deion signed with the Cowboys. When the Giants were eliminated from the baseball race in late September, Deion underwent ankle surgery. A month after surgery, Deion joined the Cowboys. He joined the Cowboys on October 29, 1995, and once again he was able to help his team reach the Super Bowl. Dallas beat Pittsburgh, 27–17, to win Super Bowl XXX.

Sanders did not play baseball during the 1996 season. He wanted to focus on football because the Cowboys decided to expand his role. He would now be one of the team's regular receivers, as well as a cornerback, and occasional return man. During the season, Sanders caught 36 passes for 475 yards on offense. Once again he was selected to the NFC Pro Bowl team for his defensive play. The Cowboys finished 10–6, but lost in the second round of the playoffs.

In 1997, Sanders returned to baseball. He signed with the Cincinnati Reds, and would be the team's starting centerfielder. He finished the season with a .273 batting average, and was among the league leaders with 56 stolen bases.

After the baseball season, Sanders returned to the Cowboys. Dallas decided to use him less as a wide receiver, but now he would be the team's punt returner. The Cowboys struggled through the regular season, finishing 6–10, and missing the playoffs. Sanders played well, and was once again selected to play in the Pro Bowl.

It is easy to misjudge Deion Sanders. Most people do. People see him strut into the end zone with a hand behind his helmet, or pump his fist in the air after stealing a base, and they think he is arrogant and foolish.

People who think badly of Deion are mistaken.

"The true me?" Deion says. "You think Michael Jackson sits in that room wearing that white glove all day long? No he don't. You think Eddie Murphy goes around cursing everybody out 24 hours a day? No he don't."[1]

Deion's on-the-field behavior is merely an act. He is being flamboyant on purpose.

"People take things out of context," Deion says. "They see me high-stepping down the field and think that's the way I am in everyday life. As if, when my wife asks me to get something to drink, I get up and high-step to the refrigerator, holding my daughter over my head. It's not like that.

"But people seem to take the way I perform on my job for the way I am in life. The truth is, I'm a very family-and-home-oriented person."[2]

Deion has a daughter named Deiondra, and a son named Deion. He and his wife have divorced. Since then, Sanders has devoted himself to his religion. He preaches at a parish in Plano, Texas.

Deion is image-conscious, everybody knows that. He owns lots of clothing. He wears plenty of jewelry. But does that make him a bad person?

FACT

Deion has his own clothing line of jogging suits, winter coats with fur collars, sweatshirts, and T-shirts. The clothes carry a "Prime Time" logo. Prices range from $16 for a T-shirt to $205 for the coat. The $125 jogging suits are available in bright orange, purple, and green combination.

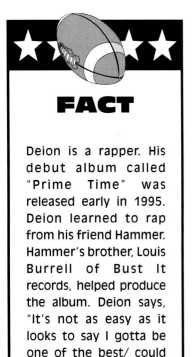

FACT

Deion is a rapper. His debut album called "Prime Time" was released early in 1995. Deion learned to rap from his friend Hammer. Hammer's brother, Louis Burrell of Bust It records, helped produce the album. Deion says, "It's not as easy as it looks to say I gotta be one of the best/ could never be less/ don't even stress/ you can't get with this kick this. There's gotta be a flow."[5]

"The only thing kids from the streets look up to are fancy clothes and cars and jewelry. So they look up to drug dealers," Deion says. "But I'm showing them something else. I got all three, and I'm proving you can do it on the right side."[3]

Deion spends countless hours speaking to children at schools across the country. One school Deion visits every year is North Fort Myers High where he graduated. He gives the football team sixty-five pairs of Nike shoes before the start of each season. One year, Deion showed up at the football field wearing a black trenchcoat and holding a telephone. Coach Wade Hummel asked Deion to give his players some advice. Deion hugged the coach and announced, "When you have this coach right here, you guys are in business." Then he spent the next hour in his trenchcoat demonstrating football moves.[4]

Deion has a vision of building a youth center. He calls it The Prime Time Kids Center. He believes a great difference can be made in a child's life with a couple of hours of adult supervision after school. Here is Deion's dream: "I want to pick the kids up in these great-looking black buses and take them to my youth center," he explains. "When we get 'em there, they're gonna do their homework, and then the ones that want are gonna have a chance to play sports. That is what got me off the streets and kept me off the streets. I want to give kids the chance to do the same thing.

"It would've been easy for me to sell drugs. But I had practice. My friends who didn't have practice, they went straight to the streets and never left. That moment after school, that's the moment I want to grab."[6]

Deion doesn't ask to be a role model. But he knows that because he is a superstar, children will use him as one. They try to imitate him on the field, or even copy his personality. And the people who truly know Deion, know there is nothing wrong with that.

"He's not anything like a lot of people perceive him," Braves third baseman Terry Pendleton says. "Everybody wants to talk negatively about him. They don't talk about the time he spends with kids. Or when he's out doing something for Say No To Drugs. Those are the kinds of things people ought to be reading about Deion Sanders—especially kids. They look up to him as a role model. He is a *good* role model."[7]

Deion Sanders is the first athlete to ever play in both a Super Bowl and a World Series. Now that he has a Super Bowl ring, he'd like a matching World Series ring.

Notes by Chapter

Chapter 1

1. Ira Miller, "Resentment Awaits Deion in Atlanta," *San Francisco Chronicle* (October 13, 1994), p. 1.

2. Ibid.

3. Ibid.

4. Ibid.

5. Atlanta Falcons 1993 Media Guide.

6. Joan Ryan, "Deion Steals the Thunder in His House," *San Francisco Chronicle* (October 17, 1994), p. 1.

7. Matt Millen, FOX-TV telecast, October 16, 1994.

8. Ryan, p. 9.

9. Ira Miller, "49ers Prove Who's Boss," *San Francisco Chronicle* (October 17, 1994), p. 1.

10. Ryan, p. 9.

Chapter 2

1. Telephone interview with Connie Knight.

2. Ibid.

3. Ibid.

4. Ibid.

5. Telephone interview with Margaret Kegley.

6. Gary Shelton, "Dim the Neon Light," *Georgia State Times* (November 23, 1990), p. 1.

7. Telephone interview with Wade Hummel.

8. Ibid.

9. Telephone interview with Connie Knight.

Chapter 3

1. Telephone interview with Wade Hummel.

2. Telephone interview with Connie Knight.

3. Telephone interview with Mike Martin.

4. Ibid.

5. Gary Long, "Flash, Bash Fuel FSU's Defense," *The Sporting News* (November 23, 1987), p. 32.

6. Ibid.

7. Florida State 1987 Media Guide.

8. Long, p. 32.

9. Brent Musburger, CBS-TV telecast, November 3, 1987.

10. Dave Scheiber, "Decisions, Decisions," *Sports Illustrated* (July 3, 1989), pp. 31–34.

11. Florida State 1988 Media Guide.

12. Curry Kirkpatrick, "They Don't Pay Nobody To Be Humble," *Sports Illustrated* (November 13, 1989), pp. 52–60.

Chapter 4

1. Bill Chastain, "Beers With . . . Deion Sanders," *Sport* (October 1990), pp. 25–27.

2. Curry Kirkpatrick, "They Don't Pay Nobody To Be Humble," *Sports Illustrated* (November 13, 1989), pp. 52–60.

3. Joe Sexton, "Sanders Dives Into Prime Time as He Makes Yankee Debut," *The New York Times* (June 1, 1989), p. 1.

4. Dave Scheiber, "Decisions, Decisions," *Sports Illustrated* (July 3, 1989), pp. 31–34.

5. Sexton, p. 1.

6. George Vecsey, "Sanders Sees How It's Done," *The New York Times* (June 6, 1989), p. 1.

7. Scheiber, pp. 31–34.

8. Larry Munson, WSB-radio broadcast, September 10, 1989.

9. Bradley, Mark, "Unchained Deion Shows His Humble Side When He Could Have Gloated in Glory," *Atlanta Journal* (September 12, 1989), p. 2.

10. Ibid.

Chapter 5

1. Curry Kirkpatrick, "They Don't Pay Nobody To Be Humble," *Sports Illustrated* (November 13, 1989), pp. 52–60.

2. Ibid.

3. Ibid.

4. Guerry Clegg, "Sanders Rates His 1st NFL Start C Plus," *Columbus Ledger-Enquirer* (October 16, 1989), p. 1.

5. Ibid.

6. Staff, "Up and Down Sanders Is Up Once Again," *The Sporting News* (July 30, 1990), p. 15.

7. Bill Chastain, "Beers With . . . Deion Sanders," *Sport* (October 1990), pp. 25–27.

8. Staff, "Sanders to Resume Two-Sport Career," *The Sporting News* (February 11, 1991), p. 33.

9. Tim Kurkjian, "Now Ready for Prime Time," *Sports Illustrated* (April 29, 1991), pp. 64–65.

10. Gene Stone, "Sanders Experiment Moving Slowly," *Gwinett Daily News* (August 20, 1991), p. 1.

11. Peter King, "It's His Call to Make," *Sports Illustrated* (October 7, 1991), pp. 90–91.

12. Mike Lupica, "The Neon Nineties," *Esquire* (June 1992), pp. 59–60.

13. Ed Hinton, "One Thing or . . . the Other," *Sports Illustrated* (April 27, 1992), pp. 38–45.

Chapter 6

1. Ed Hinton, "One Thing or . . . the Other," *Sports Illustrated* (April 27, 1992), pp. 38–45.

2. Ibid.

3. Peter King, "It's His Call to Make," *Sports Illustrated* (October 7, 1991), pp. 90–91.

4. Hinton, pp. 38-45.

5. Jim Litka, "Deion's Day," *Falcons Weekly* (November 1, 1992), p. 1.

6. Glenn Sheeley, "Sanders Brings Winning Lift to Team," *Atlanta Journal-Constitution* (October 25, 1993), p. 1.

7. Ibid.

8. Ibid.

9. Marla Ridenour, "Sanders Has Invigorated Falcons," *Columbus Dispatch* (November 25, 1993), p. 9.

10. Ibid.

11. Bryan Burwell, "Falcons' Sanders Flies into MVP Territory," *USA Today* (December 14, 1993), p. 4.

Chapter 7

1. Clark Judge, "49ers Ready for Prime Time Addition," *San Jose Mercury News* (September 15, 1994), p. 1.

2. Gary Swan, "Stylish Sanders in the 49ers' Corner," *San Francisco Chronicle* (September 16, 1994), p. 1.

3. C. W. Nevius, "Sanders Injects Needed Thrill," *San Francisco Chronicle* (September 26, 1994), p. 1.

4. Scott Ostler, "Deion Is More than Anyone Expected," *San Francisco Chronicle* (December 7, 1994), p. 1.

5. Ibid.

6. Chris Jenkins, "Chicago Can't Keep S.F. from Date with Destiny," *San Diego Union-Tribune* (January 8, 1995), p. 1.

7. Jerry Magee, "Switzer Gets Call, but It's Against Him," *San Diego Union-Tribune* (January 16, 1995), p. 7.

8. Kevin Kernan, "Mismatch—Young's Six TD Passes Throw Bolts for a Loop," *San Diego Union-Tribune* (January 30, 1995), p. 16.

Chapter 8

1. Curry Kirkpatrick, "They Don't Pay Nobody To Be Humble," *Sports Illustrated* (November 13, 1989), pp. 52–60.

2. Ed Hinton, "One Thing or . . . the Other," *Sports Illustrated* (April 27, 1992), pp. 38–45.

3. Kirkpatrick, pp. 52–60.

4. Telephone interview with Wade Hummel.

5. Kim Cunningham, "Why He's Called Neon," *People* (April 4, 1994), p. 126

6. Mike Lupica, "The Neon Nineties," *Esquire* (June 1992), pp. 59–60.

7. Frank Dolson, "Neon Deion Means More Than Just Glitz and Hits," *San Diego Union-Tribune* (August 26, 1992), p. 2.

Career Statistics

FOOTBALL

YEAR	TEAM	G	INTERCEPT		KICKOFF RETURNS			PUNT RETURNS			
			INTS	YDS	KO	YDS	AVG	PR	YDS	AVG	TDS
1989	Falcons	15	5	52	35	725	20.7	28	307	11.0	1
1990	Falcons	16	3	153	39	851	21.8	29	250	8.6	3
1991	Falcons	15	6	119	26	576	22.2	21	170	8.1	2
1992	Falcons	13	3	105	40	1067	26.7	13	41	3.2	3
1993	Falcons	11	7	91	7	169	24.1	2	21	10.5	1
1994	49ers	14	6	303	—	—	—	—	—	—	3
1995	Cowboys	9	2	34	1	15	15.0	1	54	5.4	0
1996	Cowboys	16	2	3	—	—	—	1	4	4.0	2
1997	Cowboys	13	2	81	1	18	18.0	33	407	12.3	2
TOTALS		122	36	941	149	3,421	23.0	128	1,254	9.8	17

G= Games, INTS= Interceptions, YDS= Yards, KO= Kickoff Returns, PR= Punt Returns, AVG= Average, TDS= Touchdowns

BASEBALL

YEAR	TEAM	G	AB	R	H	2B	3B	HR	RBI	SB	AVG
1989	Yankees	14	47	7	11	2	0	2	7	1	.234
1990	Yankees	57	133	24	21	2	2	3	9	8	.158
1991	Braves	54	110	16	21	1	2	4	13	11	.191
1992	Braves	97	303	54	92	6	14	8	28	26	.304
1993	Braves	95	272	42	75	18	6	6	28	19	.276
1994	Braves	46	191	32	55	10	0	4	21	19	.288
1994	Reds	46	184	26	51	7	4	0	7	19	.277
1995	Giants	85	343	48	92	11	8	6	28	24	.268
1996	DID NOT PLAY										
1997	Reds	115	465	53	127	13	7	5	23	56	.273
TOTALS		609	2,048	302	545	70	43	38	164	183	.266

G= Games, AB= At Bats, R= Runs, H= Hits, HR= Home Runs, RBI= Runs Batted In, SB= Stolen Bases

Where to Write Deion Sanders

Mr. Deion Sanders
Cowboys Center
One Cowboys Parkway
Irving, TX 75063

On the Internet at:

http://www.nfl.com/players/
http://www.dallascowboys.com/

Index

A

Aikman, Troy, 82, 84, 85

Arizona State University, 35

Atlanta Braves, 58–62,
        63–70, 75

Atlanta Falcons, 7, 9–13, 15,
        45, 51–54, 55–62,
        66–67, 70, 72–73, 75,
        77, 80

Auburn University, 38, 43

Avery, Steve, 65

B

Barfield, Jesse, 49, 50

Battle, Hinton, 20

Berryhill, Damon, 69

Blake, Arthur, 38

Bonds, Barry, 68

Bowden, Bobby, 30, 33–34

Bradley, Mark, 45, 54

Brien, Doug, 11

Briley, Greg, 48

Brock, Jim, 35

Brown, Johnny, 29

Buffalo Bills, 70

Butler, Bobby, 56

Butler, LeRoy, 40

C

Cabera, Francisco, 68

Campbell, Marion, 54

Carter, Dexter, 38

Chicago Bears, 81

Cincinnati, University of, 35

Cincinnati Bengals, 58

Cincinnati Reds, 60–61, 65,
        75, 90

Clark, Vinnie, 7

Clemson University, 40

Cleveland Browns, 72

Clutterbuck, Bryan, 50

Cook, Toi, 84

Cox, Bobby, 68, 69

Cummings, John, 18

D

Dallas Cowboys, 58, 72–73,
        77, 80–85, 89–90

Davis, Eric, 12, 82

Deer, Rob, 50

Dickerson, Eric, 56

Duper, Mark, 67

E

Erickson, Craig, 72

Espinoza, Juan, 49

Everett, Jim, 79

F

Fain, Richard, 26, 29

Favre, Brett, 40

Ferrera, Ted, 17
Florida, University of, 29, 31, 38, 42
Florida State University, 29–36, 38–40, 42–44
Floyd, William, 84, 87
Flutie, Doug, 56
Fort Meyers Rebels, 21
Furman University, 38

G

Gault, Willie, 60
Gehrig, Lou, 48
George, Jeff, 11, 13
Glanville, Jerry, 60
Grant, Mark, 65
Green, Dallas, 48
Green, Tim, 72
Griffey, Ken, Jr., 48

H

Hammer, 91
Hanks, Merton, 79, 80
Harper, Alvin, 82, 84, 85
Harper, Roger, 72
Hatcher, Dale, 53
Hebert, Bobby, 73
Henderson, Rickey, 49, 50
Heyward, Craig, 9, 11
Holman, Brian, 49
House, David, 20
House, Morgan, 20
Houston Astros, 64
Houston Oilers, 58

Hummel, Wade, 23, 24, 25, 28, 92

I

Irvin, Michael, 33, 73, 77, 82, 83, 84

J

Jackson, Michael, 91
Johnson, Gene, 42
Jones, Brent, 11
Jones, Cedric, 56, 57
Jones, Clarence, 63–64
Jones, Jerry, 89

K

Kansas City Royals, 20, 26
Kegley, Margaret, 21
Kelly, Roberto, 47, 51, 75
Kelly, Todd, 11, 15
Kirkland, Monte, 29
Knight, Connie, 16, 18–20, 29
Knight, Willie, 18

L

Leonard, Jeffrey, 49
Lewis, Richie, 31–32
Los Angeles Raiders, 60
Los Angeles Rams, 52–54, 70
Louisiana Tech University, 42
Louisville, University of, 38

M

Mantle, Mickey, 48
Martin, Mike, 29–30, 32, 34
Mason, Bill, 43

Mattingly, Don, 49

Mays, Willie, 33

McDonald, Tim, 11, 80

Means, Natrone, 87

Miami, University of, 29, 33,
    38, 39

Miami Dolphins, 66–67, 77

Michigan State University,
    36, 40

Millen, Matt, 12

Miller, Chris, 67

Milwaukee Brewers, 50

Mims, Hattie, 18

Minnesota Twins, 62

Munson, Larry, 53

Musburger, Brent, 38

Myrick, Tony, 25

N

Nebraska, University of, 38

New England Patriots, 56–57

New Orleans Saints, 70, 72,
    77

New York Jets, 66

New York Yankees, 39,
    47–51, 57, 75

North Carolina,
    University of, 33

Novacek, Jay, 84

O

Oklahoma State University,
    31

P

Pagliarulo, Mike, 48, 49

Parker, Eugene, 68

Pendleton, Terry, 93

Pittsburgh Pirates, 59,
    66–68

Pollack, Chris, 35

R

Reeves, Walter, 43

Reynolds, Harold, 48, 49

Rice, Jerry, 10, 11, 73, 74, 84,
    87

Richard, Stanley, 88

Rijo, José, 61

Rison, Andre, 9, 10, 11, 12,
    13, 15, 36, 73

Roberts, Dick, 34

Ruth, Babe, 48

S

Sanders, Deion
    childhood, 17–21, 23
    high school, 23–27,
        28–29
    Super Bowl, 87–88
    World Series, 68–70

Sanders, Deion, Jr., 91

Sanders, Deiondra, 91

Sanders, Mims, 17

Sanders, Ricky, 13

San Diego Chargers, 85

San Francisco 49ers, 7, 9–13,
    15, 61, 73, 77, 79–85,
    87–88, 89
San Francisco Giants,
    64–65, 89
Sax, Steve, 49
Schmidt, Derek, 33
Schroeder, Jay, 60
Schuerholz, John, 59
Seattle Mariners, 47–49, 51
Seattle Seahawks, 62
Siefert, George, 80, 88
Slack, Reggie, 43
Slaught, Don, 48
Smith, Emmitt, 42, 84, 85
Smith, Sammie, 35, 38
South Carolina,
    University of, 29,
    42
Southern Mississippi,
    University of, 34,
    38, 40
Steinbrenner, George, 51
Swann, Lynn, 55–56

T

Tampa Bay Buccaneers, 60,
    62, 72
Taylor, John, 10
Testaverde, Vinny, 33
Toronto Blue Jays, 68–69
Tulane Unversity, 38
Tulsa University, 30

V

Virginia Tech University, 42

W

Watters, Ricky, 10, 11, 83, 87
Williams, Dayne, 43
Williams, Kevin, 83
Wilson, Wade, 72

Y

Young, Bryant, 11
Young, Steve, 10, 11, 83, 85,
    87, 88
Yount, Robin, 50

Z

Zeno, Marc, 38
Zucker, Steve, 51